Keeping Wild Birds in Your Yard Year-Round

A Home Gardener's Guide

By Albert L. Swope

Copyright

ISBN: 9781692111571

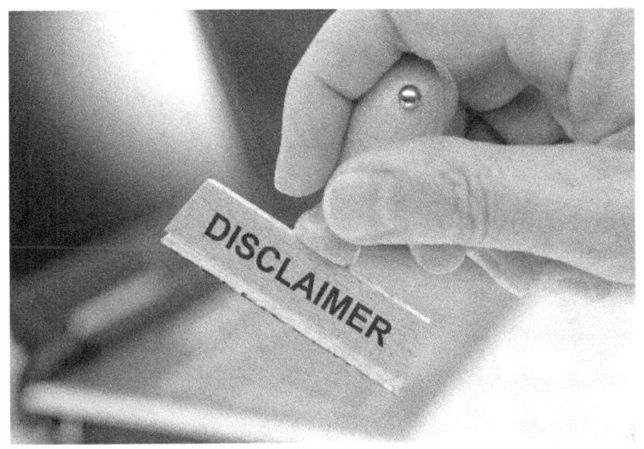

Disclaimer

No warranty whatsoever is being expressed or implied regarding the contents of this book.

Please note that the information contained within this document is for educational and entertainment purposes only. Every attempt has been made to provide accurate, up to date, and reliable information.

Readers acknowledge that the author is not engaging in the rendering of legal, financial, medical, or professional advice.

Albert L Swope

Table of Contents

Also Published By This Author

Published Books:

- Lemongrass: A Home Gardener's Guide
- The Bean: A Home Gardener's Guide
- The Chili Pepper: A Home Gardener's Guide
- Growing Sweet Marjoram: A Home Gardener's Guide
- Growing Zucchini And Summer Squash: A Home Gardener's Guide

- Cilantro and Coriander: A Home Gardener's Guide
- Growing Eggplant: A Home Gardener's Guide
- Tarragon: A Home Gardener's Guide

Blogs:

- Scientia Compendium - A collections of information technology and consulting knowledge
- Writing and The Written Word - Thoughts on reading, writing, and publishing
- The Homestead Gardener - Thoughts on Home, Garden, and Yard

Introduction

It's seven in the morning, and you've had a long night and an even more restless sleep. You wake up to the sun's rays piercing through what little space you left in your blinds, and instantly stretch and groan as you turn around in bed. It promises to be a beautiful morning, a new day full of achievement. Can you imagine the scene?

Now picture it with the beautiful sounds of chirping birds.

Not bad, huh?

Attracting wild birds to your garden can require many adjustments. Creating a bird sanctuary takes a little knowledge and effort. It is essential to understand what plants you need to grow to attract the right type of birds, and how the different seasons will affect which food sources are available.

While bird-watching will help you understand more about what birds in your area like to eat, how they feed and what sort of shelter they prefer, it is also necessary to research in advance and make sure your garden provides the necessary physiological needs that the birds will require. That means that your garden should not only provide plants as a source of food but, also, have bird feeders, birdbaths for water and bathing, as well as different forms of shelter a bird can use for nesting or roosting.

It is also important to understand how seasonal changes will affect their food sources as well as their shelter requirements to help you aid in protecting the birds during the cold winter months and providing more water during the hot, summer days.

Protecting the birds from predators will also be a reason they seek refuge in your garden as it provides the safety and security of the habitat they need.

Understanding where to place bird-feeders and birdbaths, as well as the risks that come with it in terms of pests or health issues, will also help provide solutions to these problems and prevent any harm to the birds.

Once the birds have appeared in your garden, it is important to make them feel constantly welcome by ensuring that bird feeders and birdbaths are always cleaned and filled by providing the necessary food and drink requirements to maintain a healthy source of nutrition.

Ensuring that the birds receive a balanced diet, the garden will need to attract other insect and small animals which the birds will feed on, as well as provide other sources of food and drink.

While transforming your garden into a wildlife attraction needs a lot of care and effort, it will also be a way of helping birds find food and safety to survive all year round. Not to mention, your mornings will never be the same again!

Albert L Swope

Why Have Birds In Your Yard Year-Round?

Having birds in your back yard is a sign that your garden is quite healthy. That is because the birds play a vital role in the garden's ecosystem, making sure that there's a healthy balance. While waking up to their chirping or seeing them fluttering around the garden can be quite merry, there are so many more benefits of having birds in your yard all year round.

Birds act as a natural pest control
With birds feeding on a variety of insects, they reduce the number of pests attacking your crops. Insects such as aphids, mosquitoes, spiders, and caterpillars can destroy your garden, but birds can help with eliminating these insects without the need for pesticides.

Not only will your garden be pest-free, but it will also minimize the need for pesticides, which in turn can reduce costs as well as reduce the risk of exposure to harmful chemicals in your food. When birds are present, they reduce the need to use toxic insecticides.

Birds aid in flower pollination
Your garden can be cheerful and in full bloom when keeping wild birds around. That is because certain bird species act as efficient pollinators to flowers by spreading their nectar, which helps garden flowers bloom bigger and brighter. The best thing about that is that the more flowers bloom because of pollination, the more birds will be attracted to your garden, making it a healthy, balanced eco-system. And let's not forget that this way, healthy insects such as bumblebees and butterflies will also find the garden attractive, which further aids in the pollinating process. Not only will you enjoy the chirpiness and contagious happiness of the wild birds humming around you, but you'll also feast your eyes on the beauty of wildflowers. Here are a few examples of birds that act as great pollinators:

Hummingbirds are one of the more useful birds when it comes to pollination. Because of

their slender and narrow beaks. A hummingbird's tongue also has tube-like qualities, allowing them, along with their beaks, to drink nectar from flowers.
While feeding, the pollen grains stick to their bills. As the bird moves from flower to flower, it aids in pollination.

Hummingbirds are native to the Americas and sunbirds are native to Africa, but both are an important pollinator which tends to feed on long, tubular, and red-to-orange flowers and feed on its nectar.

Orioles also play an important role in pollination as they transfer pollen from tree to tree while eating nectar from their flowers.

Birds can help in reducing weed
There are certain birds such as sparrows and finches that feed on weed seeds. That means the growth of weed is not only contained but also prevented before they even sprout. Eliminating the weed can contribute to a healthy garden by keeping it from taking over. Weed is also known for spreading quickly and having the power to destroy a perfect garden in just a matter of weeks. With these seed-eating birds, great amounts of weed seeds are consumed, helping in the control of

unwanted plants that can cause harm to the garden without having to go through the hard work and backache of eliminating the weed plants yourself.

Study local wildlife

Having wild birds around all year will give you the chance to observe the bird species that come to your garden, what they feed on, as well as their impact and how the climate affects the birds attracted to your garden. In other words, you'll have a unique opportunity of studying wild birds, migration, seasonal plumages, as well as learning about the bird's courtship behavior and nesting habits. It can also help you make changes to your garden to benefit further from the kind of birds that appear and how to accommodate their needs and ensure their survival.

Birds can be a powerful source of stress relief

There's a reason bird-watching is such a common hobby- and that is because it can be extremely helpful in releasing stress.
Watching birds, listening to their chirping and humming their songs can help get rid of a lot of stress as well as encourage you to take the time and effort to work in the garden to improve their habitat. Both the birds and the

improved vegetation will help you immerse in nature's beauty, promoting well-being.

Attracting Birds to Your Garden

Food sources For Birds

Bird-friendly feeding is one of the best ways to attract birds to your garden. According to the type of birds you want to attract, there are certain plants your garden should include to welcome the birds with open arms. However, one needs to understand that providing a habitat for the wild birds will mean that you invite other insects and animals into your garden as well to act as their food source.

Depending on your garden size, your location, and climate conditions, the flowers you decide to plant will differ immensely.

For shaded areas, a wild zone with epicedium's, periwinkles, and Solom's seal will be extremely attractive. However, if your garden is sunnier, flowerbeds that require large amounts of sunlight such as cranesbills, red valerian, and achilleas to grow will take over your garden and make it look phenomenal.

Having a small garden doesn't mean it can't be bird-friendly. It just means you should make a few conscious decisions on what to plant. With smaller sized areas, you can attract the birds by adding a few shrubs to create a thick, solid area of leaves that the birds can find shelter.

The type of soil will also help you determine what to plant to attract wild birds, as light soils will welcome annual poppies and marigolds.

Apart from plants and flowers, the grass itself is an important aspect of maintaining wildlife. Worms found in groomed lawns can be an excellent food source for birds such as blackbirds, or you can even transform part of your grass into a meadow and attract a wider diversity of birds. The meadow approach will include more insects such as anthills and grubs, which in turn makes and starlings appear.

The more flowers that attract pollinating insects, the richer your garden will be, as it will give the flowers a bigger chance of spreading, as well as give the birds a wider variety of nutrition in terms of insects and plants.

The way you plan and care for your garden will also widely affect the type of bird to which it appeals. For instance, if you decide to keep your borders growing rather than cut them back in the autumn, the plants will be a rich source of nutrition for finches and sparrows, as they provide a large number of seeds. Even if the plants are dying, they can act as a source of shelter for the birds and insects. Invertebrates find comfort in dry herbage, which is a great food source for wrens, goldcrests, and dunnocks. Even if your garden might seem a little messy, the garden will fill with birds that will add color and character.

According to the type of plants you grow, different birds will find the garden attractive.

Below are some of the plants that will attract birds to your garden.

Deciduous trees

- Mulberries attract many songbirds, robins, and cardinals due to the sweet fruits.
- Flowering Dogwood: Being a fruit that appears in the autumn, it appeals to bluebirds, tanagers, grosbeaks and other birds.
- Crabapples: This tree grows in autumn and winter, and finches, waxwings, and cardinals love its fruit supply.

Conifers

- Eastern Red Cedar: Evident in autumn and winter months, it is favored amongst – waxwings.
- Spruces: Available in the autumn and winter seasons, it is essential for crossbills and other seed eaters.

Other plants are also an essential food source for the following reasons:

Sunflowers

Planting sunflowers in your garden will not only add a cheerful, bright vibe but will also attract many birds. That's because sunflowers have masses of seeds tightly packed in the middle section that seed-eating birds find irresistible. It also provides oil-rich nourishment for finches, long-tailed tots, sparrows, siskins, nuthatches, and many other seed-eating birds. Sunflowers come in all sizes, making them adaptable to any garden spreading their bright colors and cheerful vibe.

Black Chokeberry

Attracting songbirds in fall and winter will transform your garden into a peaceful and stress-free zone. Planting chokeberries will create bluish-black fruits that songbirds adore. The plants are also a very pretty addition to the garden as they grow to be 3-6 feet tall and 10 feet wide, adding an extravagant look to your garden. Just make sure to plant them in a sunny area and that the soil is well-drained to get the best outcome.

Ivy

Common wild ivy is a great plant to enhance wildlife in your garden. That is because it attracts many insects in different seasons, which the birds use as a source of nutrition. Not only that, but when the black colored berries start to appear, the garden will fill with hungry birds such as thrushes, waxwings, starlings, jays, finches, and blackbirds as they devour the berries. Insects such as caterpillars also use the leaves for food, and other birds use them for shelter and nesting, too. It is worth mentioning that ivy plants need maintenance. While they provide thick shelters and do not require much sunlight, they only grow in well-drained soils.

Hawthorn

The berries that this plant provides is a favorite for blackbirds, redwings, and fieldfares. It appears from February to March, attracting other bird species to your garden too, such as chaffinches, starlings and greenfinches. Insects such as caterpillars and moths also feed on the leaves, which are eaten by baby birds.

Honeysuckle

For smaller gardens, honeysuckles can be a great plant as they are ideal for tight spaces. They attract many insects and aphids, which hungry birds can feed. The berries that appear in the autumn can also be a source of nutrition for birds such as thrushes, warblers, and bullfinches.

Teasel

Goldfinches, buntings, and sparrows will flock to your garden when the seed heads start to appear in autumn. This tall plant will add a lot of beauty to your garden and favored amongst these types of birds. It is distinctive in its length and best planted in the sun, but also tends to grow well in partly shaded areas with moist soil. Insects as well as birds, love this plant and feed on its flowers.

Cotoneaster

This plant is high in nectar as well as red berries, making it a source of attraction for birds in any garden. Cotoneasters are tough, strong, and resilient even in the driest of seasons, making it suitable for any climate.

They also provide plenty of berries, which are nutritious for garden birds such as blackbirds, thrushes, and waxwings. The branches are loaded with red berries in the autumn and are devoured by the birds in no time. With over 200 species of cotoneaster existing, you can easily find the perfect type for your garden, regardless of its size or location.

Guelder rose
Birds such as mistle thrushes and bullfinches are quite fond of the berries that this native shrub provides. It also makes excellent hedging and is ideal in attracting birds from November to March, as that is when its fine produce of glossy berries start to appear.

Shrub rose
Blackbirds, fieldfares, and thrushes are attracted to the rose hips produced by the hedging rose, Rosa rugosa. However, the smaller hips of the Rosa Canina can also appeal to a far wider range of birds as it stays juicy and ripe until late winter.

Fire thorn
Fire thorns provide an immense amount of winter berries, which attract all sorts of birds during the winter. They also provide shelter as they grow to a height of 500 cm and make

a great addition to the garden with their white blossoms.

Perennial asters

Seed-eating birds love this type of plant as it is lavish in seeds if it remains uncut until the spring. It also acts as a colorful border in your garden.

Sorbus

All types of Rowan produce berries that the birds are very fond of as a food source. Sorbus' grow to a height of 500 cm (16 feet) and attract many birds.

Shelter and Roosting

For the birds to survive, it is essential to provide habitats and shelter for them, especially during the harsh winter months. While there are many ways to create shelter in your back yard that won't be a hassle, there are also many natural forms of shelter that birds will seek refuge. When the birds feel safe, and find a place to reside, they will stay close and call your backyard their own home. The shelter will also help in attracting a wider variety of birds.

After the birds feed before dusk, they will want to settle down and find a roosting spot to spend the night. Providing roosting boxing in your garden will help create a sense of loyalty and reliability, ensuring the bird can count on your garden for its basic needs.

Why do birds need shelter?
Providing shelter in your backyard will be extremely beneficial for birds as it will create a place where they can feel safe as well as create nests. However, there are also other reasons why having shelter is important.

Safety
As mentioned before, the shelter provides safety, not only from the weather conditions but also from predators that feed on birds. Natural shelters will help the birds to camouflage and act as a barrier where they can hide. Hawks, cats and other predators will find it difficult to attack or hunt the birds, providing protection and safety. When the birds are nesting, it is also crucial for them to feel safe, and finding shelter will provide that sense of security.

Weather protection
While birds can survive the different weather conditions, having good shelter will allow

birds to keep warm and dry during the cold of winter. Being warm and dry will benefit the birds who will consume less energy in adjusting their body temperatures. When shelters provide insulation from rain, snow, and wind, the birds can find it a lot easier to keep warm, and survival rates improve.

Food

Natural sources of shelter such as trees and plants can also act as a food source, making it even more suitable and beneficial for birds as it provides both food and shelter. Birds can eat different parts of a plant such as buds, berries, fruits, and seeds as well as the insects that are attracted to these plants. Having a shelter that works as both an essential food source, as well as protection from predators and severe weather conditions will be a great way to keep the birds nearby.

Natural types of shelter

Plants, trees, and shrubs can be planted just as a source of shelter for the birds. Having shelter will be a great way to guarantee that the birds will stay once the plants have already attracted them. Below are some types of plants that will act as a shelter for birds in your garden.

Trees

Trees provide shelter for the birds and can help them become unreachable from predators. A well-designed landscape will have both coniferous and deciduous types of trees to ensure that there are places for the birds to create nests, sources of nutrition, as well as trees that provide shelter throughout the entire year.

Shrubs

Smaller birds and quails find shelter in shrubs and bushes. If your garden and yard are small, shrubs can provide shelter idea as shrubs come in a variety of sizes which can be selected and or adapted to smaller gardens.

Grass

Leaving the grass un-mowed will make the grass strands longer, giving small birds and insects a place to find shelter when needed.

Tree cavities

Hollow trees with cavities in them can be an excellent shelter for nesting birds. The cavities also make a great hiding spot for roosting owls.

Plants

Many plants form a dense protective place due to their length and sturdiness which allow the birds to hide. They sometimes start as small plants and grow into larger trees, allowing shelter in all its growth stages.

Cypress plants

Cypresses come in many different variations with over 80 types. They can be tiny dwarfs of under 50 cm (20 inches) or can grow to become humungous trees. Making Cypresses great for roosting and nesting and shelter for many birds.

Other types of shelter
There are also human-made shelters, such as roost boxes and nest boxes that provide birds with a safe and secure place to stay warm during the night. There are many types of human-made shelters available but putting up a variety of human-made shelters several locations around your yard. Thus, encouraging a variety of birds to make themselves at home.

Feeding and Feeder Care

Foods for different birds

Different varieties of birds have different dietary needs and type of birds, and feeding requirements may change as birds migrate and weather patterns change with the seasons. The Changing in birds types and weather changes can more pronounce the farther north you live.

Hummingbirds

Wherever hummingbirds find good shelter, water, and source of food, they'll make a home. In effect creating a colorful environment by planting certain flowers, shrubs, and trees in your yard, making nectar in your kitchen to supply their feeders and installing fountains within sight of the feeders such that the fine mist they provide enables the birds to bathe and cool off, attracts Hummingbirds. Attending to these preferences will, in the long run, bring a birder much fun and entertainment as he regularly watches the flying maneuverings of hummingbirds.

Attracting hummingbirds

You can attract hummingbirds by providing an environment, which contains the colors, flowers, trees, and vines which hummingbirds prefer. Use of perennials will reduce the gardening and landscaping work each year and provide a permanent incentive for the hummingbirds to return. Additionally, planning your landscaping and gardening to provide cross-seasonal flowering plants will provide food sources and attractors for hummingbirds in addition to any feeders you may be providing.

Colors that Attract Hummingbirds

Hummingbirds love brightly colored flowers and plants such as red, pink, orange, and purple with red being their favorite color. Hummingbird gardens should be awash in red feeders and decorations, in addition to more natural touches like flowers.

Common Flowers that Attract Hummingbirds

When planning a garden to attract hummingbirds, the color and type of flowers with nectar-availability are of prime importance as these keep Hummingbirds coming back to their favorite feeding spot.

Hummingbirds are attracted to tubular-shaped flowers like the shrimp plants, California fuchsia, pineapple sage, and cigar plants because these accommodate the hummingbirds' long beaks as they drink nectar. Flowers that bend downwards (nodding flowers) like the Mexican bush sage, fuchsia and columbine also attract Hummingbirds, because the disposition of these flowers make it easier for any hovering bird to drink nectar.

Annuals, biennials, and flowers that bloom at different times of the year, such as the bee balm, mint, peppermint, cardinal, zinnia, lupine, petunia, and columbine planted in the garden. The flowers should be spaced out to make for easy maneuverings of the hummingbirds among flowers.

Trees Which Attract Hummingbirds
Hummingbirds need places to perch and rest from their flying. The male hummingbird also needs to perch as he guards both his space and food source; hence, the need to have trees and shrubs in the garden. Some trees and shrubs that attract Hummingbirds include

the eucalyptus tree, red buckeye, strawberry tree, and tulip tree.

How to Provide Hummingbirds Nesting Area

Hummingbirds build their nests on forked, leafy trees and shrubs usually 5 – 15 feet above the ground. These trees not only provide good anchors for the nests but also prevent the wind from blowing the eggs and nestlings out into the open air. Trees like the willows, black cottonwood and mulberry provide the needed shade for the nests.

- Plant red flowers and decorate the yard in red, which can be as simple as tying ted ribbons to ends of branches near feeders for hummingbirds to investigate.
- Provide well maintained and regularly refilled hummingbird feeders.
- Provide a misting water source
- Provide humanmade nesting mounts.

Human-made Hummingbirds Nesting Mount

You can create a hummingbird nesting mount by:

- Create a forked shape ('Y') by attaching two dowel rods. Install it under the eaves

and attach a leaf-sized sheath of plastic, 2 inches above the Y-shaped rod to give a sense of shelter.
- Leave spider webs intact as hummingbirds use the strands to hold the nest together and as anchors to tree branches.

Feeding Hummingbirds

Hummingbirds eat a variety of diets, but its main food source is nectar. With a few steps, a birder can feed hummingbirds by hand:

- A birder should colorfully have arranged feeders and flowers in one location to familiarize the birds with their feeding spot.
- Be there every day at their most popular feeding times observing their behavior.
- Sit some distance away from the feeders but gradually advance towards the feeders daily.
- Sit still each time – no sudden moves or sounds, so they are not scared away.
- Be consistent with your behavior day by day, so they get used to you.

Homemade Hummingbird Food

while commercial hummingbird food is fine, homemade is cheaper, plus they can serve as a stopgap until you can get to the store if you prefer to use commercial hummingbird.

How to Make Hummingbird Food

The basic hummingbird nectar recipe attracts Hummingbirds mostly because it is just like the natural sucrose content of high nectar-producing flowers. It is also a nutritious and easily digestible energy source for

Hummingbirds. Here is a nutritious hummingbird nectar recipe:

- Combine a solution of one-part ordinary white sugar and four parts filtered water in a clean stovetop safe saucepan.
- Bring the hummingbird food sugar-water combination to a gentle boil and boil for about five minutes.
- Remove from the heat, and allow to cool.
- Once cooled, place in a sealed storage container that portion which you will not immediately place in your hummingbird feeders and store in the refrigerator.

How To Store Hummingbird Food

Hummingbird food once cooled, should be placed in a clean container with a tightly sealed lid and stored in the refrigerator. Since hummingbird food will be refrigerated, you may make a large enough batch for several refills of your hummingbird feeders. However, do not make so much you cannot use it within a couple of weeks.

Hummingbird feeder placement

Hummingbird feeder placement is important for a couple of reasons. First, to protect the food from unnecessary direct sunlight and heat. Secondly, to make it convenient for the hummingbirds to use and find.

- Feeders should be hung in partial shade, away from direct sunshine. Partial shade ensures that the nectar does not overheat, ooze, and drip off the feeder.
- Hang hummingbird feeders near a natural food source.
- Additionally, it has been my experience that hummingbird feeders placed near a place to roost are more utilized, and will allow the hummingbirds to hang around longer if they can roost protected in a nearby tree.
- Hummingbirds, at least in my backyard, tend to be a little territorial and will protect feeders, so, you will want to distribute them a fair distance apart so that no one hummingbird can monopolize the food source.
- You may want to consider only partially filling your hummingbird feeder until you see what the actual consumption is, perhaps, something like 1/3 to 1/2 full. You may use less and reduce the chances of the nectar spoilage.

When To Change Your Hummingbird Food
Several factors can dictate how frequently to change your hummingbird food. Among them are:

Daytime high temperatures: basically, the hotter it is, the more frequently you will need to change your hummingbird food prevented from spoiling. An approximate guide would be:

Daytime high temperatures	Frequency of change
61-80	4-5 days
81-90	3-4 days
90 and above	Daily or every other day

When hummingbird feeders become contaminated by other animals, for example, dead ants or bees floating in your feeder.

The visual inspection which reveals the something doesn't look quite right with the feeder liquid.

Additionally, if it appears the hummingbirds are not using a particular feeder, something may be wrong, so, you may want to clean the feeder and change the feeder location.

How to Maintain Feeders

Proper maintenance of your feeder is important to prevent unnecessary food spoilage and poison your hummingbirds. How often hummingbird feeder needs cleaning will depend somewhat on the weather. The hotter of the weather, the more frequently hummingbird feeder should be cleaned.

- Feeders should be cleaned every 3 – 4 days, and more often in hot weather using bottle brushes.
- One could use a mixture of sand and water to shake out molds from areas that brush cannot reach. Feeders should be rinsed with hot water anytime there's nectar-change.
- Harsh detergents should never be used to clean feeders.

- If you feel like you need to sanitize your hummingbird feeder with a strong vinegar-water mix would be best.

Best Ways to Stop Bee Raiders
Bees, both honey, and native, can be serious raters and hazards for your hummingbird feeder. Not to mention they can scare off and bother the hummingbirds are trying to attract. To discourage bee raiders, especially, during drought periods when bees may raid your feeders more actively, here are a few pointers:

- Bees are attracted to yellow. Any yellow item decorative features on feeders need to be removed or painted over with red.
- Lids and stoppers of feeders should be secured and put in shaded areas to avoid leakage due to expansion.
- Droppings of nectar by the birds on the ridges of the feeder should be wiped off at once.
- Use feeders with holes at the top, not the middle or near bottom provide a better barrier to honey bees. Use feeders with holes at the top work best if the hummingbird food is a fair distance below the feeding point, where the bees cannot reach it but the hummingbirds can.

How to Stop Ants
Ants can be a serious pass to your feeders.
Not only are they annoying, but they can
climb in and drowned in the feeder liquid and
pollute the food for the hummingbirds. Protect
your hummingbird feeders from ants:

- Feeders should be hung in partial shades,
  away from direct sunshine. Partial shade
  helps to prevent the nectar from
  overheating, ooze and or drip off the
  feeder.
- Feeders should be hung with a fishing line
  so that ants do not easily grip the thin,
  slippery line.
- Install ant guards as they serve as barriers
  between ants and feeders.

Cautions

To keep from harming your hummingbirds
and keep your population healthy here are a
few tips:

- Use pure unadulterated filtered water, if
  available.
- Never use honey or artificial sweeteners in
  hummingbirds' feeders as it has the
  potential for mold formation and may
  cause the birds a paralytic infection that
  could be fatal.

- Avoid the using pesticides on flowering plants in your garden, because the pesticides can enter the flower nectar and sicken the birds.
- Avoid adding red dye to the hummingbirds' nectar.

Feeding Hummingbirds in Spring

If you want to attract hummingbirds, the best way is to provide a consistent supply of nectar, but birders often ask when is the right time to put out hummingbird feeders to allow the birds savor the free meal. Various factors determine the ideal time to start feeding hummingbirds in a particular area. To avoid wasting your nectar and the birds don't suffer from lack of food; it's important to understand these factors as well as the peculiarities of your area regarding hummingbirds.

Determinants of When to Feed Hummingbirds

When they are around all-year-round, there is no particular time to bring out the feeders. However, many hummingbirds are migratory, which means they are not around to enjoy the free meal at certain times of the year. Hummingbirds' migratory behavior varies from place to place, and this in addition to the following factors affects when they arrive in your yard for treats.

Location: Hummingbirds are present year-round in many parts of South America and the Caribbean as well as some southern and coastal regions of the US and Mexico. In such areas, every time is the best time. For other regions, the ideal time to put out hummingbird feeders is determined by the local hummingbird population and the season.

Climate: In early spring, hummingbirds love to be in places with a mild or warm climate. People in these areas should start feeding hummingbirds as early as possible to provide them a consistent nectar source. In places where the temperature is cooler and during late spring, birders can delay putting out their hummingbird feeders. The geographical location and elevation can influence the climate of an area, and this can impact the ideal time to start feeding hummingbirds.

Migration: Another way of identifying when to put out hummingbird feeders is to study their migratory behavior. When they are migrating, hummingbirds require good nectar to recharge their bodies and any fresh, clean feeders will readily become their host. The presence of a reliable feeder can be a boon for early migrants because it may be their only source of food at a time when flowers are not yet in full bloom.

When to start feeding hummingbirds

There are no exact dates to begin feeding hummingbirds, but their migratory patterns and the time they begin visiting feeders are reliable.

Year-Round Feeding

Year-round feeding is possible where hummingbirds reside year-round or in areas where overwintering birds join local hummingbirds during the winter months. Year-round feeding is common along the Pacific coast of the United States and Southern British Columbia as well as southern and central Florida, southeastern Arizona, and the Rio Grande Valley area in south Texas because hummingbird populations are available year-round.

February and March

In the United States, hummingbirds start migrating early. Birders in the deep south and northern Florida can begin feeding hummingbirds as early as mid-February to early March.

March and April

By mid-March through early April, early migrant hummingbirds on their way to breeding grounds further north start landing in the central United States. Rufous hummingbirds and ruby-throated hummingbirds are some of the first arrivers, and they would be glad to find your feeders in the backyard.

April and May

By late April and early May, hummingbirds start appearing in their northern ranges. Backyard birders should try to make their feeders available with fresh, clean nectar by the first week of May.

May and June

Hummingbirds reach the northernmost part of their ranges by late spring or the beginning of summer. The birders in the Alaskan territory of the rufous hummingbird and the central Canadian range of the Calliope hummingbird can still wait until the middle of May or early June to start feeding hummingbirds. But watch out for early arrivers and put out the feeders for them.

Regional Tips for Feeding Hummingbirds
Look for these clues to determine the best time to put out hummingbird feeders in your locality:

- Swelling tree buds or early flower blooms heralding the beginning of spring,
- The arrival of birds like buntings, warblers, and other migrating neotropical bird species,
- Information in regional records of the first arrival of hummingbirds or local sightings,
- Information birding journals about the arrival dates of hummingbirds in the past.

Like other migrant birds, the arrival and departure dates of hummingbirds are easy to predict. Despite yearly variations of a few days, the best way of determining when to put out hummingbird feeders is to study their migration patterns.

It's better to be early than late
Putting out hummingbird feeders too earlier instead of too late is the best rule of thumb when deciding the ideal time to start feeding the birds. When you start seeing the first hummingbirds, it may already be too late to attract the earliest migrants by then. Hummingbirds are blessed with excellent

geographical memories and will continue to return to your feeders every year once they find them. While you might need to make arrangements to keep the nectar from freezing during the winter or replace spoilt old nectar once or twice, the trouble pales in significance to the joy of hosting these beautiful birds at the arrival of every spring.

Bluebirds

If these gorgeous birds make an appearance in your garden, you'll be the envy of many birdwatchers out there.

Bluebirds mainly eat insects as they make up 68% of their diet. While bluebirds eat most insects, grasshoppers, beetles, crickets, spiders, and caterpillars are their absolute favorites. However, they also get part of their nutrition from berries and fruits, especially during the winter months when insects are scarce, the berries can make up to 50% of their diet. Here is a list of plants that not only attract bluebirds but can also act as a food source:

Plants:
- Holly
- Black Cherry
- Crabapple
- Red mulberry
- Flowering Dogwood
- Hawthorn
- Mountain Ash
- Red Cedar Sumac

Shrubs:
- Blackberry
- Blueberry
- Chokeberry
- Bayberry
- Elderberry
- Cranberry
- Pokeweed
- Hackberry
- Firethorn
- Winterberry

Vines:
- Grape
- Virginia Creeper

Bluebirds are very fond of mealworms, which can are available at bait shops, pet stores or bird supply stores. These are the larval stage of darkling beetles. They can be raised quite easily and don't serve any danger to humans. To ensure that bluebirds are getting the nutrition they need, here's how to prepare mealworms:

- Put bedding of cornmeal or wheat bran into a plastic container with some ventilation such as drilled or punched holes at the top.
- Add a piece of potato, apple, or carrot to create a moist atmosphere inside the container.
- Any excess mealworms should be refrigerated to avoid them turning into adult beetles.
- Once it is feeding time, it is best to serve mealworms in a shallow dish; however, it is recommended to avoid using wooden containers as mealworms can escape from the rough surface.

☐ Place the mealworms in the feeder and always use the same signal to inform the bluebirds that their food is ready. Serve mealworms once or twice a day, depending on the number of birds you're feeding. The approximate serving size will be around 100 worms.

Sparrows

A sparrow's diet is mainly vegetarian; however, newly hatched sparrows need protein to promote growth and good health. A newly hatched sparrow's diet consists mainly of small insects such as caterpillars and aphids. The adult sparrows will also eat small insects during this time to be able to feed their little ones. To maintain high levels of energy and high metabolic rates, sparrows will most commonly eat food rich in vitamins, oils, and nutrients.

Seeds and plants
Sparrows mainly eat seeds with white millet being an absolute favorite. However, red millets are also heavily devoured by these birds. Because of their small beaks, medium-sized seeds and grain are best for feeding sparrows.

Having bird feeders with bird seeds in your garden is also a great way to guarantee that the sparrows are getting the food sources they require and will make an appearance in your yard. Corn and black oil sunflower seeds are most commonly used in home bird feeders and tend to attract quite a lot of sparrows. Corn and black oil sunflower seeds help sparrows preserve their energy levels into nesting and roosting and staying warm rather than trying to find a source of food. Sparrows also find certain tender plants quite appealing, such as grasses and soft buds.

Fruits and vegetables
While fruits and vegetables aren't an essential part of the sparrow's diet, they tend to peck at bits and pieces, but do not eat the whole thing. It is quite common to find holes in berries and other fruits, and therefore, it is

important to secure your produce from being ruined.

Bread
If seeds aren't available, the sparrows are more than happy with bread crumbs and other foods which are thrown out by humans. They even tend to seek out the garbage and rummage for food that humans have left unwanted.

Goldfinch
A Goldfinch is a delightful bird to have around your garden. Beautiful and colorful, Goldfinches are a sight for sore eyes. Feeding this lovely bird is not a difficult ordeal.

Seeds

A goldfinch's diet consists primarily of seeds. That is why small growing plants such as dandelions, groundsel, thistles, and teasels are essential to provide a convenient food source for these birds. Their long, slender beaks are designed to make prizing seeds from the flower heads an easy task.

To ensure you have enough food to provide for Goldfinches, designate a part of your garden as a feeding sanctuary. A feeding sanctuary can be made by growing certain plants and having feeders with bird seeds for them to be able to feed on all year round, particularly from November to March when seeds from flowers and plants are scarce.

Plants

Planting colorful plants will also be easier for goldfinches to spot. Flowers such as sunflowers, cosmos, daisies, marigolds, and poppies provide seed heads that are appreciated by goldfinches. However, one of their absolute favorite flowers is the black oil sunflower as it has smaller flower heads, making it easier for the goldfinch to handle. It is also advisable to refrain from deadheading flowers to allow these birds to feed on them for a longer time. Flowers such as coneflower and sunflower can provide seeds on their stalks throughout the entire summer and can be used as a good source of nutrition during the winter by cutting and saving excess flower heads.

Trees and shrubs

Trees and shrubs which provide a goldfinch with a healthy diet are white alders, big leaf maple, Chinese elm, western red cedar, river birch and island mallow amongst various other options. The seeds from these sources are enjoyable for goldfinches, as well as the buds from alders, cottonwoods, oaks, sycamores.

Thrushes

It is not common to find these songbirds in your garden; however, attracting them means that you've managed to create a safe space that is bird-friendly. That doesn't mean it isn't impossible, but it is essential to understand what thrushes' diets are composed.

Insects
Due to the diet of Thrushes being composed mainly of insects, worms, and snails, reducing the use of insecticides in your garden to provide more natural food sources for the birds. That way, instead of having to use chemicals to eliminate the pests, the birds will find the garden appealing and will use these insects as a source of nutrition, eliminating the problem at the same time. During spring and summer seasons, a vast amount of insects is needed to provide a source of protein for the new hatchlings to grow and become healthy.

Plants
While insects are the main priority in terms of food for thrushes, when insects are hard to find during fall and winter, thrushes seek berries and fruits to be able to survive. Planting different types of berries around your garden will give the thrushes a food source, as they like to eat raspberries, grapes, and elderberries.

Feeders

It is also possible to provide other sources of food in the feeders situated in your garden. The feed can include soaked raisins, kitchen food remains, as well as small pieces of suet. When the weather gets tough, and food is scarce, thrushes will even resort to feeding on oil-rich seeds to get the energy levels they need to survive and keep warm. Filling up the feeders with seeds during these months will ensure that the thrushes have something to eat.

Wrens

Another common wild bird that would be a great addition to your garden is a wren. Just like all the other birds, wrens have a specific diet that needs to be adapted and prepared for wrens to appear; however, even with the food, it is still difficult to attract these charismatic birds to your garden. Here are a few tips to attract Wrens:

- Grow plants that will act as a double source of nutrition by providing both insects and berries.
- Provide food in areas that are densely covered, as wrens are known to be shy birds.
- Avoid using insecticides, to lure the insects to your plants and therefore have an important food source for wrens.
- Add mealworms, suet, and even peanut butter to your feeders, as wrens tend to be curious and will be attracted to these food sources.
- Peanut butter and suet can even be spread on tree trunks or branches to encourage wrens to visit.

A wrens' diet consists primarily of insects, but will also resort to berries when insects are scarce. Having shrubs that provide both a dense area for the wrens to hide and rummage for food is an excellent way to attract these birds. These shrubs can include blackberries and beauty berries as they provide shelter and great hiding spots, too.

Changing Food Regularly

When using feeders, it is vital for the sake of keeping the wild birds around that the food is regularly available. That is because the birds will only consider your garden to be a reliable source of food if they find a source of nutrition they can feed on every time they visit.

So, how often do the feeders need to be filled?

Depending on several factors, how long the bird feeders take to empty varies. Among factors are:

Feeder size and capacity
There's a wide variety of feeders available in the market. Depending on your garden type, space, and location, the appropriate feeder can come in different sizes and capacities. Feed volumes one of the factors that can vary greatly over time as the supply of natural food changes.

Type of food
Whether the feeders consist of seeds or mealworms will also have a great impact on the duration necessary for food to be changed out. For example, the mealworms will also need to be changed out if not eaten, as they will develop into adult beetles. Due to their size, they also take up more space, which will mean that fewer birds will be able to feed on them.

Number of feeders available in your backyard
The amount of food you need per feeder will also highly depend on how many feeders you have in your yard. If you only have one, then it should be bigger, have a larger quantity of food, and changed at least 2-3 times per day (or every time it is emptied) to guarantee that a supply of food is always available. However, food spread amongst several feeders, even if

one bird feeder runs low, the birds will be able to feed out of the others feeders.

Amount of birds using the feeders

The number of birds feeding in your backyard will also affect how often the feeders need to be changed and how frequently the consumption. It is also a good idea to notice if the number of birds is increasing to be able to provide sufficient food.

Weather patterns

The weather can impact how often the birds use feeders for food. How often the birds use feeders will also depend on where your feeders are situated and if they provide shelter for the birds. That way, even during the harsh weather, the birds will be able to feed without struggling for their safety and trying to keep warm.

It is also essential to take notes of the types of birds that use the feeders and what is their main source of nutrition. That is because there are certain seasons when their food sources are scarce and therefore, will rely upon seeds or other which feeder can provide. Increasing the amount of feed required and the speed at which the feeder will need replenishment.

Feeding times

Once you've realized which birds have taken an interest in your garden, the feeding times will differ. That would mean that the feeders will need to have a constant supply during the birds' specific feeding times.

Accidents and spills

It is also important to realize how efficient your feeders are and whether they are appropriate and user-friendly for the birds your garden is attracting. Depending on the feeder style and the birds that are using it, you could find that many accidents and spills take place, which requires replenishment.

Fresh seeds

Keeping seeds fresh will also encourage birds to be loyal to your feeders, as they do not like spoiled seeds that have been kept out for a long time. Regularly changing the seeds will ensure that the birds favor your feeders and become loyal to them. It is also essential to replace moist seeds to prevent mold and fungus from forming.

Feeder attractions

Birds are curious beings and are attracted to anything unusual or out of the ordinary. Having a colorful, lively, and active feeding station will appeal to their curiosity.

Cleaning Frequency

With many birds using the feeders daily, regular cleaning of bird feeders is essential. So, here are a few birdfeeder cleaning tips:

Frequency
- Feeders should be cleaned at least four times a year to ensure that the hygiene level is in check for the birds.
- If the seeds get wet, it is important to throw them out, clean the feeder, and replace the seeds with new, fresh ones.
- Sick birds can spread diseases and so, once they're spotted, the feeders should be cleaned to avoid other birds from getting sick too.
- It is best to wear gloves while cleaning the feeders, even though it is unlikely that any diseases or infections will spread to you.

While cleaning bird-feeders might seem like a tedious task, there are good reasons for keeping clean bird feeders:

Attracting other species
When a feeder is dirty, it emits a foul smell that in turn, can attract many other unwanted

species such as insects, mice, rats, or wildlife that can compromise the safety of the birds.

Grease and debris

A dirty feeder can also be harmful to the garden as it can result in debris and grease. A dirty feeder can cause damage to your flowerbeds and lawns. Mulching under underneath bird feeds can be helpful. Using a natural mulch (not stones) which can be removed, disposed of, and replaced will help to keep the area around the bird feeders clean and beautiful.

Many Birds Feed on the Ground

There are times when accidents happen and the seeds from the bird-feeders spill, leaving it accessible for birds to feed on the ground. Other birds feed directly from the grass, flowers or insects hidden inside the ground, making it a common feeding station. That is why it is also crucial to ensure that the areas where the birds feed are cleaned thoroughly to keep the birds healthy.

- Remove old or wet seeds from underneath feeders.

- Make sure that there is no rotten fruit in the trees where birds feed.
- Always have mulch or some sort of insulation beneath feeders to cover bird droppings.
- Regularly keep birdbaths, fences, and feeders clean.

Prevent molding of feed

After severe weather conditions, the feeders will likely become moldy. Especially on the bottom of the feeders, beneath the seeds. To prevent the molding of feed and to ensure a safe environment for the birds:

Cover your birdfeeders

Having a shelter for your birdfeeders will help prevent the rain or snow from reaching the birdfeeders and creating mold. Instead of placing them in the middle of the garden, you can strategically place them underneath a roof or thick tree that protects it from the rain.

Drainage

Some birdfeeders come with drainage options. That way, the water collected will be released through the drainage and prevent the mold from surfacing.

Mesh

Having mesh will allow ventilation into your birdfeeders and therefore permit the air to flow in, making the moist areas evaporate quickly.

Inspection and Cleaning

Regular inspection, clean and drying of bird feeders are good ways to ensure the quality and safety of your bird feeders. Also, the inspection, clean and drying of bird feeders is an opportunity to commune with your bird friends and to inspect the bird feeders for any necessary repairs or need for replacement.

Water Sources for Birds

Having water sources in your garden can be even more beneficial to birds than food. That is because all types of birds need water, not only to cool their body temperature but also to remove dust, parasites, and debris from their feathers.

Birdbaths

Having birdbaths is one of the easiest, most common ways of adding water to the habitat created for birds. Birdbaths are available in a variety of designs, but the most common ones are the following:

Pedestal: With a strong base, holding an elevated dish 3-4 feet above the ground, this style of the birdbath is one of the most common. Pedestal birdbaths come in various materials such as plastic, metal, glass, ceramic or concrete. It can come in quite a few decorative designs, colors or artistic touches, with some of them even consisting small fountains.

Dish: The simplest option is to use any shallow bowl as a basic bird water dish, which can be placed at different levels. The shallow bowl can be placed on the ground, on a tree branch, stump, steps, or even on the patio. There are even hanging dishes models to hang on the wall, fence, or post.

Heated: When the weather gets cold, a heated birdbath becomes necessary. If you already have a birdbath, an immersible heating accessory can be added to prevent you from having to buy a new birdbath with a heater.

Tips to consider when using birdbaths:
- Pick the birdbath location wisely. Choose an area that is shaded, but isn't too close to shrubs where predators can be hiding.
- Birdbaths should be between 1-3 inches deep but tilted to the sides.
- Avoid using concrete birdbaths as they don't withstand the freezing weather and tend to crack.
- Look for a dish that can be easily cleaned and has a diameter of at least 2-feet for more than one bird to be able to use it at a time.

- Place a couple of rocks in the dish for birds to have different levels to stand on.
- Pick a dark-colored basin as the reflection is higher, making it easier for birds to spot.
- Water should be replaced every 2-3 days to stay clean. If the water contains algae, mud, or droppings, the birds will stop using it.
- Adding an accessory such as a mister or dripper can not only keep the water fresh but also attract birds to the noise and movement of the accessories.
- Birds have difficulty flying when wet. That's why the birdbath should be placed strategically with a nearby space where the birds can sit and preen after a bath.
- Clean birdbaths with a stiff brush using a cleaning solution of 9 parts water to every 1-part bleach. It is best to leave the birdbath in the sun after it is washed to help remove the dark spots.

Running waters and fountains

Birds are curious species and are attracted to any motion or sound. For that reason, having a waterfall or fountain can not only be a beautiful addition to your greenery, but also an ideal way to attract birds to the garden and supply water for them. A human-made waterfall works by using a pump that recycles water. Seeing moving water is one of the most appealing aspects for birds and can be quite easy for them to spot from a distance. With the water constantly moving, it also makes the running water cleaner than staying still; however, it is still essential to change it out every once in a while, as clean water is necessary for all kinds of birds.

When thinking of adding a fountain, there are so many designs that can be very appealing for birds. The pump used to recycle the water can make the water flow, fall or even splash, drip, or flow into streams. The pump power affects the flow capacity and speed of the water as well as the strength in which it flows, varying from a simple spray to a more energetic waterfall.

Fountains come in a large selection of sizes, styles, and shapes, according to the design you're interested in as well as the size that would fit your area. Fountains also vary greatly from an aesthetic perspective. It is quite common to find small sculptures such as butterflies, flowers, birds, frogs, turtles, or dragonflies and or use geometric patterns and color.

How to take care of a birdbath fountain:
Birdbath fountains can be easy to clean and take care of if installed correctly. Keep these tips in mind, and your fountain will be in the best possible condition:

- The fountain should be placed at least 15 feet away from a birdfeeder to avoid the pump getting clogged with seeds or debris.

- Add a small net to the pump to regularly get rid of trash from the fountains to enhance its functionality.
- Stop using the fountain before the winter period to avoid the water from freezing.
- Clean and dry the fountain thoroughly before storing it for the winter to avoid any damages.
- Maintain the functionality of the pump by checking water levels regularly and adding water as needed.

Yard Ponds, Water Gardens, and Creeks

There's something about water that feels so relaxing. Whether it's flowing or stationary, having a source of water in the middle of the greenery will not only beautify your backyard but will also increase the number of birds that flock to your garden. While birdbaths are the most common, adding a water source can make a huge transformation and attract more wildlife to your area. That's where water gardens and ponds come in. With many different options in shapes, sizes, and designs, a simple pond can still serve the purpose, look quite attractive, and attract more wildlife without going overboard in terms of budget.

What type of wildlife do you want to attract?

The kind of wildlife do you want to attract must be considered before you start planning your wildlife pond. That is because according to the species you want to attract, the design and function of the pond will completely differ.

Birds

If the pond is used primarily to attract birds, it can be rather small and shallow to allow for birds to bathe. It would also require shallow rocks or sand to create a rough surface to prevent the birds from slipping. Accentuating the pond with a waterfall will make it more attractive for the birds and easier for them to spot.

Insects

Wildlife ponds attract insects such as dragonflies, damselflies and water striders, too. When the insects appear, there will be a larger source of food for birds, too making the pond useful for more than just drinking and bathing.

While amphibians and fish can also be part of wildlife ponds, they require different characteristics and a lot more maintenance to ensure that the water is clean and therefore it is best to provide a separate water source for birds.

When designing a pond, there are a few questions to consider to help you create the most appropriate pond for your garden as well as for the birds you wish to attract.

How much space can the pond take up?
First, determine how much space is available in your backyard to be able to build a pond. While a small pond can be efficient in its purpose of attracting wildlife, most people tend to wish they'd gone bigger. Consider the space that can be used and determine the size accordingly without the pond taking over your entire garden.

How much runoff might it receive?
Placing the pond should be in an area that doesn't receive runoff from other lawns or roads. That is essential to avoid herbicides, fertilizers, insecticides, and other sources of contamination that can affect the water's cleanliness.

Is the area level?

When choosing an area for your pond, it is best to make sure that it is steady and level. That is because a level site is not only easy to design, but also to maintain.

How much sun does the pond area receive?

Having an area that is part shade is necessary to avoid overheating and excessive algae growth in the water. The sunlight required by your pond will depend upon the type of plants used in the pond.

Is the pond located in a safe place?

The location is essential, not only to determine the sunlight coming in but also to guarantee the safety of the birds that will use it. It is also necessary to ensure that there are no electrical lines underneath the soil to prevent any disasters from happening. A pump, as well as any other electrical features, will also need to be verified and in compliance with the necessary electrical fittings. Installing any electrical items will require an electrician to guarantee that the pond is safe.

Will special water features be added?

The designs of backyard ponds and water gardens can include waterfalls, dripping fountains, and recirculating streams. It is best to decide what characteristics you'd like to create in your pond to be able to factor in the requirements while digging the pond.

Will plants be added to the pond?
Another important decision to make is the kind of plants to be added to the pond if any. That is necessary to understand the necessities the plant will require in terms of sunlight, space, location, and maintenance.

Albert L Swope

The Necessity for Clean Water

Drinking water

Clean water is essential for a bird's health and survival. Birds need water as a drinking source as well as to ensure their cleanliness and prevent diseases. Because birds have no sweat glands, they require less water than other animals. But that doesn't mean they don't need water. Birds still tend to lose water through respiration and in their droppings. That's why during the winter months when water sources are frozen, and summer months when the hot weather tends to dry up most water sources, having a clean drinking source is essential.

Birds also get some of their required liquid intake from their food as well as by drinking. Fruits and nectar are favored amongst birds and contain a lot of water sources, which could amount to up to 90% of their required liquid intake. However, birds that rely mostly on seeds for nutrition have a dry diet and need to drink more water.

While water is available to most birds in the form of ponds, streams and even drops of dew on leaves in the early mornings, it is hard to guarantee that these water sources of water are clean enough for them to drink.

Providing clean drinking water is a great way to help birds preserve their energy levels and also keep them constantly coming to your garden, as they know they will find the food and water they need.

Water for bathing

Another reason clean water is essential in a bird's day-to-day life is to be able to bathe. Keeping the feathers clean by bathing is an essential part of maintaining the feathers in good condition. When a clean water source is available, a bird can take a quick dip, which allows it to dampen the feathers, making the dirt far less difficult to remove and the feathers easier to preen.

Once the birds have bathed, they find a safe area to preen by carefully rearranging the feathers. They also release oil from the preen gland which they spread over the feathers to remain waterproof and create an insulating layer of air to keep them warm.

If clean water is extremely vital for birds, how can the water be kept clean?

A birdbath must be cleaned regularly to reduce the health risks to birds. The water should also be changed frequently to provide fresh, clean water. That's because when the water gets dirty, a layer of algae, bird droppings or even dead leaves will be visible, preventing the birds from using the water entirely, or putting them at risk of catching diseases. Removing the water and washing the birdbath thoroughly once a week will remove signs of algae or other dirt and ensure the cleanliness of the water. To remove algae can use diluted disinfectants; however, it should be rinsed out carefully to prevent the chemicals from mixing with the clean water that the birds drink.

Protection of Birds

Protection from quarrels

While birds are usually cute, pretty little creatures, they can be a real version of 'angry birds' when they need to be. Birds are very loyal and protective creatures that no matter what their size, they are willing to pick a fight if they sense any form of danger.

A nesting bird has the task and responsibility of not only protecting its nest from any signs of harm but also its eggs or hatchlings. The parental instincts that kick in can be quite dangerous, and that's why it is best to create a safe place where the birds can find shelter and build their nests without having to fight off any predators. Natural shelters such as trees and shrubs can be strategically positioned away from harmful predators to reduce the risk of quarrels.

It is also possible to create different shelter options for birds in your garden to prevent different species from quarreling over territory. When food is scarce, some birds tend to fight other birds for food as they claim a particular area to be their own. It can even be visible when a bird is found fighting its reflection, thinking that it is another bird that has come to share the food sources.

Divide the garden into different sections with foods grouped according to bird feed type. That way, each part will have its food source as well as shelter to build their nests safely without birds having to quarrel over territory.

Smaller wild birds also need protection from birds of prey such as hawks, eagles and falcons. Bird feeders with small openings, keep out bigger birds and also creating shelters and cavities that are just big enough for small birds and in areas that can shield and camouflage the small birds, keeping

small birds protected, and making it difficult
for the predators to spot the smaller birds
when hunting.

It is also important to keep any cats away, as
they tend to scare the birds. A cat can be kept
indoors or at least only be allowed to access
a certain part of the garden to prevent it from
harming the birds. It is also necessary to keep
feeders and birdbaths at an elevated distance
to guarantee the safety of the birds while
feeding and drinking. That way, they will be
far from a cat's reach and be able to fly away
safely.

Squirrel-Proof Feeds

While squirrels are cute, furry animals, they can also be quite destructive. When a squirrel takes an interest in your bird feeder, it not only eats the bird seeds and scares the birds away, but it also ends up destroying the bird feeder itself with its chewing.

There are numerous measures which can be taken to prevent the squirrels from reaching and destroying the bird-feeders.

Spice Up your Birdfeed

Adding Capsaicin to birdfeed can also discourage squirrels from raiding bird feeders.

There are commercial products which do this, like "Squirrel Away," but you can easily achieve the same result at home by coating you birdseed with hot sauce and letting the hot sauce dry on or mixing your birdseed with hot chili pepper powder. In both cases, it can be the least expensive you can find, but the important rule is -- the hotter, the better. This spicing up of the birdseed does not bother the birds, but it does make it unpleasant of the squirrels to pillage the bird-feeders.

Use the 5-7-9
Squirrels are known to be excellent climbers, even on metal poles. However, they generally can't jump higher than 5 feet off the ground, more than 7 feet horizontally and are always afraid and hesitant when it comes to dropping down 9 feet down. When placing a feeder, it is best to consider these measurements and place it at a distance where a squirrel won't be able to jump vertically, horizontally or drop down from due to its nature. That way, the feeders will be squirrel-proof and leave the birds to feed in peace.

Add a squirrel baffle
If you cannot place a bird-feeder in an area where the squirrels will not be able to reach it, then the next best option will be using a baffle. A baffle is an item that is added on to

the bird-feeder pole to prevent the squirrels from moving upwards. Squirrel baffles come in many different sizes and shapes, but most commonly look like an upside-down funnel which holds the squirrel in its center, preventing it from reaching the bird-food, as it cannot climb past the baffle. A baffle can be purchased online or from a bird or pet store and easily adjusted on to the bird feeder pole.

Keep the bird feeder's area clean
One of the reasons squirrels are attracted to bird feeders can be due to the mess and smell when the bird feeder is dirty. It is essential to constantly clean up the bird feeder as well as the surrounding area from not only scattered seeds or food but also from bird droppings. That way, the squirrels, as well as other pests, won't be attracted to the bird feeders and prevent the birds from having to quarrel with a squirrel or fly away from fear.

Repurposing toys
An interesting, yet effective way to keep squirrels away is by using toys to keep them out of bird feeders. Repurposing toys can be as simple as adding a slinky onto the bird feeder pole which not only prevents the squirrels from climbing up but also changes the direction of their path, dropping them

down on to the ground every time they use it. While a squirrel may enjoy the game, it will not be able to reach the food and will allow the birds to be safe from pests as well as squirrels.

Create a ground-level feeding station

If keeping the squirrels away is only for the sake of the birds, then the best solution is to create different ground-level stations for birds to use. That way, it will be much easier to reach, and the seeds dispersed amongst the birds, who can feed in a different area.

Use a PVC pool

While squirrels find it rather easy to climb metal or wooden poles, some materials are difficult for squirrels to climb. The slippery nature of a PVC or plastic pole will reduce the risk of squirrels reaching the bird feeder.

Controlling the squirrel population

When squirrels make an appearance in your garden, there's a lot more risk of damage to your wildlife than one might expect. That's why it is important for the sake of the birds, as well as the plants to control the squirrels and keep them away.

To keep squirrels out of your garden, avoid plant trees and shrubs which nuts and fruit which are popular food sources for squirrels. Avoid trees like the oak, acorns, hickories, pecans, walnuts, butternuts, and beechnuts. Also, avoid fruits and berries, which will provide autumn and winter food sources for squirrels such as wild cherry, osage orange, wild grapes, persimmons, mulberries, crabapples, and hackberries.

Please know that squirrels do not respect property boundaries; however, squirrels will tend to go where their food is plentiful and easiest to consistently access.

Keep squirrels away from bird feeders
While squirrel baffles are a great way to stop them from reaching bird feeders.

Place bird feeders strategically where a squirrel is unable to reach by ensuring that it is 6 feet or more off the ground or take the necessary precautions by using baffles, plastic pipes or any medium that will prevent its movement towards the birds.

Another idea is to use a squirrel-resistant feeder that circulates when a heavy body comes close, making a squirrel lose balance and fall off.

Protect plants from squirrels
Once a squirrel finds that is unable to feed or find shelter in your backyard, it will eventually resort to venturing out to find food. That's why it is also important to protect your plants and trees, too. Using a two-feet wide and six feet tall metal sheet or baffle around tree trunks

will keep the squirrels from climbing up. However, it is important to keep the sheet loose to allow the tree to grow.

It will also be useful to use a wire fencing around the vegetable gardens to keep out the squirrels and cover newly planted bulbs with mesh wires and mulch.

While there are ways of keeping out squirrels by trapping or shooting them (in a rural area). While poisons can be used to control squirrels, it is best to avoid poisons because poisons can also be harmful not only for the squirrels but for other wildlife, pets, and children in your garden.

Areas Away From Pet Traffic and Attack

Cats will hunt wild birds and kill then death. While it is impossible to train your pet to be civil to wild birds, there are steps which can be taken to protect the birds in your garden.

Feeder and birdbath placement
One way to protect the birds is by placing the feeder and birdbath in areas where the cat will be unable to reach. Keep a distance of ten to twelve feet away from any possible hiding places where a cat might be waiting to pounce. While birds need cover and places to

hide, they also need open spaces to be able to spot cats and fly away. The height and material of the bird feeders will also make it difficult for the cats to attack. Placing a bird feeder higher will make cat attacks more difficult; especially, if cats cannot climb on or near the bird feeder.

Put up a fence
Using a fence with small mesh wire or closely space metal or other non-climbable fencing material around vegetation areas where birds feed, as well as birdbaths and feeders, will help reduce the risk of a cat attack. While cats are natural climbers, having a very high fence will prevent them from jumping over and using a slippery or non-climbable fencing material will reduce a cat's abilities to climb. Regular trimming of a cat's claws will make it harder to climb and to catch and hold birds.

Use a collar bell
While a collar bell might not be a permanent solution, using a collar bell can still warn the birds that a cat is coming and give them a head start to fly away to safety.

Providing shelter for birds

Having a place where birds can find shelter in your garden is one of the reasons they will stay. Having their basic needs easily accessible will create loyalty and allow birds to consider your garden home.

Protection from harsh weather
When the weather conditions are intolerable, birds also need a place to hide, stay safe, and keep warm. Natural as well as human-made shelters can protect birds from harsh weather

Planting trees, shrubs, and bushes that provide cover from the rain and snow will allow the birds to stay safe during the harsh, cold winters. Many of these plants will also be used as a food source, as they provide seeds and fruits as well, making it easier for the birds to use them for both shelter and food.

Birdhouses and roost boxes can be a great way to ensure that the birds will be safe during the cold winters. They provide security, comfort, and warmth. They can also accommodate more than one bird at a time. While roost boxes are better sources of shelter, birdhouses can still be efficient for a roosting bird for the night and are far better than no shelter at all.

When placing birdhouses or roost boxes, it is important to position them in an area where they can make use of solar energy as well as be safe from the strong winds. More sunlight will keep dark-colored shelters and birdhouses warmer. In southern climates, shade to keep shelters and light-colored birdhouses cooler.

To ensure the birds' safety, it is also necessary to keep them away from a predator's reach by placing them away from poles or trees that can be reachable. Another option is using baffles to prevent the predators from climbing up to where the birds have sought refuge.

Nesting
To encourage birds to reside in your yard, place nest boxes that they can use for shelter, roosting, or nesting. Next boxes allow the birds to breed and give their children a safe place to grow.

When choosing where to place your nest box, pick an area that is quiet, away from sunlight, and also safe from predators and weather conditions. It is also smart to place quite a few different types of nests around the garden to see which box they prefer and which location is more suitable to set up a nest.

While providing nests will be helpful, it is also a good idea to plant hedges with dense covers where birds can create their natural nests without compromising safety.

Seasonal Care of Yard Birds

Tips for birds by season

The weather conditions have a huge impact on what needs to be placed or added in a garden to encourage wildlife, especially when it comes to birds. Climate can affect the kind of plants that grow, where to place nest boxes, how many times food should be re-filled as well as many other factors. Each season comes with its requirements to ensure that wild birds will be available in your garden all year round.

Autumn

In Autumn bird provide food sources during the autumn season is that birds need to build a reserve to get the energy required for migration.

It is a common belief that birds don't need feeding during the autumn, since having a reliable source of food will not encourage birds to migrate. The truth, however, is that the food will only aid in giving them the necessary energy needed to migrate. Certain bird types must resort to warmer climates, as they cannot withstand the cold.

It is also necessary to fill bird feeders to ensure a reliable source of food for the birds that remain during the winter.

Making sure bird food is always available in your feeders is beneficial for the following reasons:

- Local birds will be able to get their fat reserves for energy to be able to migrate.
- Bird feeders will provide an available source of food for any migrating birds that happen to pass by.
- Bird feeders will also provide food for winter birds that will remain in the area.

When autumn strikes, it is also important to make sure that there are no damages from the summer months and that your bird feeders are in good condition and will be able to sustain the winters.

It is also essential to pick autumn plants that not only offer evergreen cover but also provide lasting berries, nuts, and fruits for the autumn and winter. Other essential tasks that must be taken care of during this season is adding a heater to the birdbath and keeping it filled to prevent it from freezing early.

During autumn, the leaves of many trees and plants tend to fall, and while it might seem like common sense and intuition to remove the leaves and clean up, it is advisable to keep them in place as they provide shelter for birds and insects.

Winter

During the harsh months of winter, the weather conditions can become unbearable, increasing the risk of death in severe conditions. To preserve the safety of the birds and eliminate that risk, there are a few ways that your garden can help save their lives and get them through the winter.

Most birds tend to feed on seeds as insects and fruits are scarce during the snowy weather. For birds survive cold weather, a birds diet must consist of high fat or oil content to provide sufficient energy to survive the winter. That's why black oil sunflower seeds, peanut butter, white millet seeds and suet mixes with seeds and fruits are very nutrition for birds during this time.

In winter increase the number of and the number of times the food is re-filled as the birds will rely on the feeders as the main source of nutrition. For that reason, you want to consider when setting up your winter feeders:

- To protect the seeds and prevent the seed from being buried in snow or becoming rain-soaked and rotting, it is best to have a wide overhead cover over the feeder
- Place the feeders in a sheltered location under a hedge or roof to provide shelter and protection for the birds as they feed.
- Having feeders that take a large capacity of seeds will be more useful for the winter as it does not need frequent filling; however, it also depends on whether the climate affects

the seeds as moist seeds will cause mold and can lead to diseases.
- ⁈ Regular bird feeder Cleaning is necessary to provide safe, healthy food and to discourage rodents like squirrels.

Spring

During the spring, birds tend to mate, and with all the energy that goes into that, they require a steady source of nutrition to preserve their energy. While most flowers tend to blossom in the spring, the fruits only start to appear in the summer, making food still scarce during these periods. That's why it is essential to provide just as much food in the bird feeders as the winter months to ensure the birds' survival.

Another option is to provide birds with mixed dried mealworms and suet kibbles so they can also be able to feed their young with the nutrition they need to grow. Having these options in a bird feeder will enable the birds to get both their required protein and fat intake. It is also useful to provide fresh fruit if accessible, as the weather is still good enough that it won't go bad quickly; however, seeds and fruit blends are still a good option, too. Other sources of protein are protein-packed nuts, which can be added to any bird feed blend to create a healthy nutrition source for the birds.

Summer

During the summer months, the birds will have a selection of foods available in the garden and will make a regular appearance if they feel your garden provides them with the food they like to eat. For some birds, this can be different forms of berries and fruits while other birds need protein and will come looking for insects in your garden to feed.

Foods with high protein are required to be able to sustain the high energy levels of the summer months. If these aren't available in terms of insects, it is essential to provide the birds with protein and high-fat sources in the bird feeders, too. High-fat bird feed sources can include food such as black sunflower seeds, raisins, mild grated cheese, mealworms, waxworms, mealworms, and oatmeal. Occasionally, it is a good idea to cut slices of pears, bananas, and grapes and place them in the feeders where it is accessible for birds.

However, it is best to avoid foods such as peanuts, fats, and bread, as feeding them to their nestlings could cause harm because

their bodies are unable to digest them and can cause them to choke.
While hummingbirds enjoy nectar, it is a favorite amongst many birds in the summer, too, because it is a sugar liquid form that provides a high level of energy and satisfies the need for water.

To prevent the seeds from spoiling, place the feeders under shelter, as well as bird-baths to prevent the water from evaporating quickly.

Conclusion

Making a garden bird-friendly isn't an easy task, but it comes with many rewards. Putting in the effort to grow the necessary plants that wild birds will find attractive, as well as provide the appropriate shelter, will not only change according to the season but to the different types of birds you want to attract, too. However, the benefits are not only restricted to having wild birds singing and humming in your garden; it will also allow you to feast your eyes on the beautiful sanctuary you have created.

Understanding what each bird eats, and attracting plants and insects to your garden, will help create a balanced-eco system in your garden and eliminate the need for pesticides, as birds do the job themselves.

While plants act as a food source for birds, it is also necessary to ensure that the water supply the birds drink from and bathe in is constant. That way, their health is guaranteed, and offering both food and water will save the bird's energy levels, allowing it to focus on keeping warm.

It is important to understand that maintaining the garden all year round will require a lot of effort. For your garden to become a reliable, and comfortable destination birds can consider home, you will need to constantly provide feed, especially when it is scarce during certain seasons.

When providing food, their health is also in your hands, as the bird feeders need to regular cleaning to prevent sick birds from spreading diseases. It will also reduce the risk of healthy birds picking up diseases because of dirty feeders with mold and old seeds.

Birdbaths will also need regular cleaning, adding to your responsibilities. Unclean water is not only harmful to their health but will also be unapproached by birds. Unclean water could leave birds without a place to drink and bathe in your yarding, which is where you want the birds to be.

To avoid a reduction in the bird population because of severe weather conditions, create shelters out of natural plants, as well as providing nest boxes where the birds can create their habitat. Shelters and birdboxes protect birds from the rain and snow and are have a place for roosting or nesting. When birds decide to nest, they need a safe, warm location away from predators, where they can breed and raise their young. Providing that in your garden can help increase their population and keep the birds from abandoning their nests, leaving their young to die.

Maintaining your garden does not always mean mowing the lawn and cutting the trees, as these aspects can help create shelter for birds and promote the wilderness in which they seek comfort. Understanding what the birds need to survive, and making your garden the perfect habitat to suit their environment, will guarantee that your backyard has wild birds all year round.

www.ingramcontent.com/pod-product-compliance
Lightning Source LLC
Chambersburg PA
CBHW061359250726
48657CB00004B/1570